ENGLAND

Alice Harman

WAYLAND

FACT CAT

Get your paws on this fantastic new mega-series from Wayland!

Join our Fact Cat on a journey of fun learning about every subject under the sun!

First published in 2014 by Wayland
© Wayland 2014

Wayland
Hachette Children's Books
338 Euston Road
London NW1 3BH

Wayland Australia
Level 17/207 Kent Street
Sydney NSW 2000

Produced for Wayland by
White-Thomson Publishing Ltd
www.wtpub.co.uk
+44 (0) 843 208 7460

Editor: Alice Harman
Design: Rocket Design (East Anglia) Ltd
Fact Cat illustrations: Shutterstock/Julien Troneur
Other illustrations: Stefan Chabluk
Consultant: Kate Ruttle

A catalogue for this title is available from the British Library

ISBN: 978 0 7502 8433 2
ebook ISBN: 978 0 7502 8557 5

Dewey Number: 914.2-dc23

10 9 8 7 6 5 4 3 2 1

Wayland is a division of Hachette Children's Books,
an Hachette UK company.
www.hachette.co.uk

Printed and bound in China

Picture and illustration credits:
Alamy: A. P. S (UK) 6; British Cycling: 17, Chabluk, Stefan: 4; Dreamstime: Danielc1998 1, Clinton Moffat 10, Martin Applegate 18, Justin Black 19, Georgios Kollidas 21; Getty: Getty Images 16; Shutterstock: Neil Mitchell 5, Alex Yeung 7, Daniel J. Rao 8, hramovnick 9, Kamira 12, 21, Gordon Bell 13, Eduard Kyslynskyy 14, Bildagentur Zoonar GmbH 15, fulcanelli cover, nazlisart cover; Superstock: Prisma 11; Wikimedia: 20.

Every effort has been made to clear copyright.
Should there be any inadvertent omission,
please apply to the publisher for rectification.

The author, Alice Harman, is a writer and editor specialising in children's educational publishing.

The consultant, Kate Ruttle, is a literacy expert and SENCO, and teaches in Suffolk.

FACT CAT FACT

There is a question for you to answer on each spread in this book. You can check your answers on page 24.

CONTENTS

WELCOME TO ENGLAND

England is part of the United Kingdom, which is also called the UK. The United Kingdom is a country made up of England, Scotland, Wales and Northern Ireland.

The United Kingdom is in Europe. Can you name another country in Europe?

North Atlantic Ocean

SCOTLAND

North Sea

NORTHERN IRELAND

Newcastle

Blackpool Leeds York

Irish Sea

Manchester

Sheffield

IRELAND

Liverpool

River Trent

River Severn

Birmingham Norwich

WALES

ENGLAND

Bristol River Thames

London

Southampton

Plymouth

BELGIUM

English Channel

FRANCE

United Kingdom

EUROPE

London is the **capital** city of England. The River Thames runs through London, and there are 34 bridges over it. The most famous one is Tower Bridge. It was built more than 120 years ago.

The centre part of Tower Bridge can be lifted to allow tall ships to pass underneath.

FACT CAT FACT

Around 8 million people live in London. People come from all over the world to live there. More than 300 different languages are spoken in London's schools.

CITIES AND TOWNS

Most people in England live in cities and towns. Cities are usually bigger than towns. There are 51 cities and 935 towns in England.

York is a city in north-east England. It has a very large, famous **cathedral**.

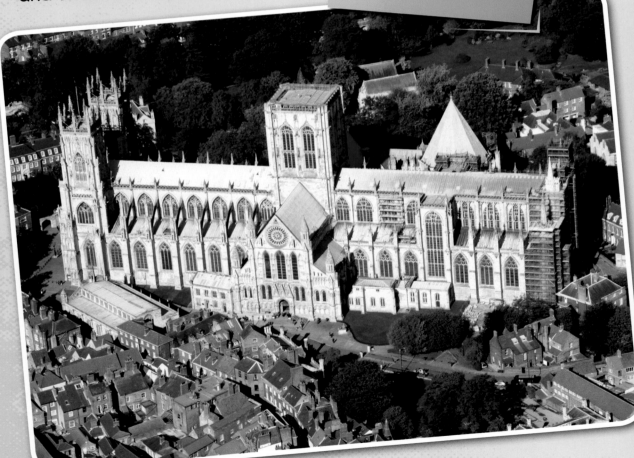

A river runs through the city of Liverpool. Can you find out the name of the river?

London is the biggest city in England. Five of the country's other largest cities are Birmingham, Manchester, Leeds, Liverpool and Sheffield. Most of these cities are in the north of England.

FACT CAT FACT

Birmingham is an English city, but 30 other places around the world also have the same name. There is a **crater** on the Moon called Birmingham!

COUNTRYSIDE

Although England is a small country, it has many types of **landscape**. There are lots of forests, but there are also large areas of grassy land.

England has some large areas of **moorland**. Can you find out where one area of moorland is?

A lot of England's countryside is used for farming. Some farmers grow **crops** such as wheat, potatoes and sugar beet. Others keep animals such as sheep, chickens and cows.

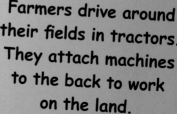

Farmers drive around their fields in tractors. They attach machines to the back to work on the land.

FACT CAT **FACT**

The **hedgerows** between fields are very important for England's wildlife. Around 1500 different insects, 65 birds and 20 **mammals** live or feed in hedgerows.

9

THE COAST

England has a long coastline. This means that there are long areas of land that are next to the sea. There are sometimes high cliffs along the coast.

cliff

These cliffs are part of the Jurassic Coast, which is in south-west England. Find out what is special about the cliffs there.

FACT CAT FACT

Cliffs are often made of a soft white rock called chalk. When seawater and wind hit the cliffs, the chalk breaks off easily. Over many years, this makes large holes in the rock called **caves**.

People live in towns and villages all along the coast. Many **tourists** like to visit the coast for holidays, especially in the summer.

Blackpool is a seaside town in the north-west of England. It has a theme park, three **piers**, a very tall tower, a wide sandy beach and donkey rides!

FOOD AND DRINK

England has lots of **traditional** dishes, such as **shepherd's pie** and fish and chips. On Sundays, people often eat a roast dinner. This is a meal of meat, potatoes and other vegetables.

Many people in England enjoy eating foods from other countries, too. This market sells food from all over the world.

Different places around England make traditional types of cake. English people often like to have their cake with a cup of **tea**.

A cream tea is a pot of tea and some scones with cream and jam. Find out which two areas of England are famous for their cream teas.

scone

cream

FACT CAT FACT

A Victoria sponge is a cake that is enjoyed all over England. It is named after Queen Victoria, who ruled England around 150 years ago. Queen Victoria liked to eat a slice of this cake for an afternoon snack.

WILDLIFE

England has 24 **native** types of mammal, such as badgers, foxes, deer and hedgehogs. Many of these animals live in woodland areas, where there are lots of trees.

Badgers dig long **tunnels** underground, with wider spaces where they sleep and eat. Find out what these underground homes are called.

FACT CAT FACT

In the past, wolves, bears and **lynxes** all used to live in England. They all died out because people **hunted** them. Some people now want to bring them back.

Many animals in England like to live in and around **ponds**. Frogs, toads and newts can stay in the water or on the land. They eat **minibeasts** such as pond snails, water boatmen and pond skaters.

heron

Other animals such as birds, grass snakes and **water voles** look for food around ponds. Herons eat frogs, fish and small mammals.

SPORT

Men and women in England like to play and watch football, rugby, cricket and tennis. England's football team first played a match more than 140 years ago, against Scotland.

There is a special cricket competition between England and **Australia**. Try to find out what it is called.

People take part in mountain biking competitions across England. Cyclists ride through forests and down hills.

Cycling is becoming more and more popular in England. There are different types of cycling, from racing to mountain biking. People enjoy riding their bikes on special **cycle paths**.

SIGHTS

The United Kingdom has a Queen, called Elizabeth II. When the Queen is in London, she lives and works in Buckingham Palace. She does not rule the country, but she welcomes important visitors.

Buckingham Palace has lots of guards around it. Many people come to watch the guards marching to music.

Stonehenge is a group of huge stones in south-west England. It was built more than 4000 years ago. The wheel hadn't been invented yet, so people had to drag the stones into place.

No one knows what Stonehenge was used for. Some people think that it was a type of calendar. Do you know what a calendar measures?

FAMOUS PEOPLE

Florence Nightingale was a nurse who became famous for caring for soldiers at war. She helped to make hospitals cleaner and safer for ill people.

Florence Nightingale lived around 110 years ago. She was the first woman to have her picture on a **banknote**.

Globe Theatre

The Globe Theatre in London looks like a theatre in Shakespeare's time. It mostly puts on Shakespeare's plays. Find out the names of three of his plays.

William Shakespeare is one of the most famous writers in the world. He lived around 400 years ago, and he wrote 38 **plays**.

William Shakespeare

FACT CAT FACT

Shakespeare invented 1700 new words and used them in his plays. Without Shakespeare, the English language would not have the words 'lonely', 'eyeball' and 'road'.

QUIZ

Try to answer the questions below. Look back through the book to help you. Check your answers on page 24.

1 How many types of native mammals are there in England?

a) 120

b) 6

c) 24

2 In a cream tea, what are scones served with?

a) honey

b) jam and cream

c) cheese

3 How many piers are there in Blackpool?

a) 3

b) 1

c) 7

4 London is the biggest city in England. True or not true?

a) true

b) not true

5 On which day of the week do people in England often eat a roast dinner?

a) Saturday

b) Tuesday

c) Sunday

6 William Shakespeare was a famous scientist. True or not true?

a) true

b) not true

GLOSSARY

Australia large country in the south-east of the world

banknote piece of paper money that can be used to buy things

capital the city where the govement (the group of people who lead a country) meets

cathedral large, important church

cave natural hole in the rock or the ground

chapel small building where Christians go to pray as they would in a church

crater large, bowl-shaped hole in a surface, often caused by something hitting it very hard

crops plants that are grown for food

cycle path path made for riding bikes, where no cars are allowed to drive

hedgerow row of bushes and other plants that separates fields

hunt to chase and kill an animal for food or sometimes for fun

landscape what an area of land looks like because of its natural features, such as trees or mountains

lynx wild animal that looks like a big cat and has soft, spotted fur

mammal type of animal that has hair and feeds its babies with milk

minibeast small animal such as an insect or a spider

moorland land where grasses and low, thick plants grow and there are not many trees

native originally from an area, rather than brought in from somewhere else

pier long platform that starts on the coast and continues out over the sea

play story that is acted out by people on a stage

pond small area of water surrounded by land

shepherd's pie dish made of lamb and some vegetables with a thick layer of mashed potato on top

tea hot drink made by pouring boiling water over leaves from the tea plant

tourist person who is visiting somewhere for a holiday

traditional describes something that a group of people have done or made the same way for a long time

tunnel long, narrow underground passage

water vole small animal that looks a bit like a fluffy rat and lives near water

INDEX

ANSWERS

Pages 7–21

page 7: River Mersey

page 8: North York Moors, Exmoor and Dartmoor are some large areas of moorland, but there are others too.

page 10: In the cliffs on the Jurassic Coast, you can see different layers of rock that show how the Earth changed millions of years ago. There are also remains of plants and animals that lived at different times in the past.

page 13: Devon and Cornwall

page 14: setts

page 16: The Ashes

page 19: A calendar measures how many days of a year have passed.

page 21: There are a lot of plays to choose from, but some famous ones are: Hamlet, Romeo and Juliet, Macbeth and A Midsummer Night's Dream.

Quiz answers

1   c)
2   b)
3   a)
4   a)
5   c)
6   b)

OTHER TITLES IN THE FACT CAT SERIES...

SPACE

978 0 7502 8220 8

978 0 7502 8221 5

978 0 7502 8222 2

978 0 7502 8223 9

COUNTRIES

978 0 7502 8212 3

978 0 7502 8213 0

978 0 7502 8215 4

978 0 7502 8214 7

WAYLAND